Loves of My Life

Loves of My Life

Holly W. Schwartztol

Although the author has made every reasonable effort to ensure that the information in this book is correct, the author does not assume and hereby disclaims any liability to any party for any loss, damage, or disruption caused by errors or omissions, whether such errors or omissions result from negligence, accident, or any other cause.

Copyright © 2025 by Holly W. Schwartztol

All rights reserved. No part of this book may be reproduced or transmitted in any form or by any means, electronic or mechanical, including photocopying, recording, or any information storage and retrieval system, without permission in writing from the author.

ISBN: 978-1-6653-1146-5 - Paperback
eISBN: 978-1-6653-1147-2 - eBook

These ISBNs are the property of BookLogix for the express purpose of sales and distribution of this title. The content of this book is the property of the copyright holder only. BookLogix does not hold any ownership of the content of this book and is not liable in any way for the materials contained within. The views and opinions expressed in this book are the property of the Author/Copyright holder, and do not necessarily reflect those of BookLogix.

Library of Congress Control Number: Pending

∞This paper meets the requirements of ANSI/NISO Z39.48-1992 (Permanence of Paper)

1 1 1 2 2 5

Dedicated to Our Panera Lunch Ladies

Holly Schwartztol's following poems have received recognition from the Pirate's Alley Faulkner Society 2024-2025 competition:

Short List
Pronounce Your Words

Finalists
Corner of My Heart

Semifinalists
Loved One Losing Memory
Memory Lingers

Contents

I Could Write a Book

Writer's Alibi	3
Sight of Night	4
Familiar Feeling	5
Older Age	7
Pronounce Your Words	8
Mammogram	9
Your Memoirs	10

Defying Gravity

Moving, 2021	15
Moving on Again	16

No Good Deed

Seller's Remorse	21
Cast Aside	22
Memory Lingers	23
Family Unrest	25
Baby Talk	27
Dorothy's Wisdom	28
Long Term Headache	30

Empty Chairs at Empty Tables

For Sharon Wendt Wesch	33
Living in a Strange World	35
Going . . .	36
Leaving	37
How Can It Be?	38
For Bob Pimm on the Death of His Father	40
Little Sister	41

Lost SFWA Voices (South Florida Writers Association)	43
Loved One Losing Memory	45
Sad Soul	47

Because I Knew You

For Barry Morris	51
For Stephanie Carter	53
Meeting Again	54
Words Interrupted	56
Who Is, Was Barry Kaplan?	58
Tales of Lee and Me	60
Corner of My Heart	61
Sweetness	62
Dining on Friendship, 2022	63
Grandpa and Daddy	64
Panera Ladies Update	65

Some Enchanted Evening

Was It Chance?	69
The Love of Robert	70
Do You Know?	71
Our Story	72
Meant to Be	73

Somewhere Out There

Pandemic Panic	77
Florida Peril	79
Pandemic Love	80
Night Frights	81
Deliver Us from Evil	82
Criminal Neglect	84
Blind Sight	86
Empty Ships	88
Hugging	90
Holidays, 2020	91
New Year's	92
Missing Grandchildren	93

Three Pandemic Haiku   94

Politics and Poker

Time to Go	97
No Reason	98
Miscounts	99
Balance Restored	100
Eve of Election, 2024	101
Day After Election, 2024	102
Inauguration Day, 2025	103
Loss of Reason	104
American Pope	105

Seasons of Love

Gifts of Gratitude	109
Never Lost	111
Twelve Days and Nights . . .	113
Psoriasis Bane	114
Call to the Medium	116

Acknowledgments   *119*

I Could Write a Book

Writer's Alibi

My mind says sit and write
and though it really isn't right
my fingers often betray me
when my laptop's tempting key

Takes me to Pogo's Jungle Gin
where I so frequently win
word Whomp might beckon
not really writing I'd reckon

And my cell phone's no better
A sure temptation go-getter
my attention it will catch
luring me to Strike-A-Match

These games form my addiction
keeping me from writing fiction
whiling away countless hours
as they seduce me with their powers

Sight of Night

Seems to be my plight
late into the night
wondering what shall I write?

Wishing a brand new story
would come in a burst of glory
nothing scary or gory.

Asking my muse what's next
more than emails or text
so I won't be eternally vext

Familiar Feeling

The writing is the easy part
when I consider how
I might struggle for a word,
a poetic line, or plot to avow

Second and third drafts
editing and such
may at times
vex me very much

And getting ready
for publication
can bring about
beads of frustration

Seeing final project in print
tickles my fancy
makes me feel giddy
and want to sprint

Waiting for others to read
fills a particular need
for recognition and
now I may plead

With friends to
promise to buy
my poems or novels
not make me sigh

When the book
awaits buyers' attraction
it's then when I begin
this age-old reaction

Recalling the topic
of my doctoral dissertation
the sadness creeps in
I lose some elation

Post-partum depression
for the new baby creation
as I tune in to feelings
of a familiar sensation

Older Age

Time to turn the page
as I face my older age
as the cauldron bubbles
with new found troubles

More than I'd had in mind
these challenges I find
health problems galore
what more lies in store?

And the world as it spins
paying for mankind's sins
bringing excessive heat
torrential rains to our feet

What's happened to truth?
from politicians uncouth
will fascism take reign
in this world gone insane?

If I'm to survive
with whatever will arrive
I'll have to learn to deal
no matter how I feel

Pronounce Your Words

When I hear them say realator
I cringe and purse my lips
I suspect an English whore

Same when I hear jewlery
my insides take a flop
to hear such tom-foolery

The one who says Febuary
makes my old teeth clench
are they from the brewery?

And the word isn't libary
can't they even read?
it's not that I'm contrary

Mammogram

Clearly the very worst
kind of test
is the one to examine
the breast

Always they want me to
have more pix
as I imagine what kind
of fix

Will be in store for me
I can't rest
my poor heart careens inside
my chest

I sigh with much relief
when I hear
you're perfectly fine, we'll see you
next year

Your Memoirs

The fragrant ember
sparking early days
what you can remember
through sunlight's brilliant rays

Your school chums
summer vacations
your dad and your mum
old train stations

Struggles in school
or the teacher who saw
when you felt like a fool
you're much more than your flaws

Perhaps you felt left out
of the playground's games
memory has such clout
like old picture frames

Tales of your first wheels
from a bike to a car
like old movie reels
with you as the star

College romances
so full of light
studies and dances
was this Mr. Right?

Details of celebrations
not easily known
for next generations
to have a touchstone

Into your feelings and thoughts
with all you've been through
battles you've fought
in the times you grew

What you write here and now
your children will see
your words will allow
a special intimacy

It's not so bizarre
as your best legacy
to keep your memoir
under lock and key

Defying Gravity

Moving, 2021

Moving on to Yuma
from Huron Avenue
need a sense of "huma"
no matter what you do.

It's not every day
A son is called to serve
the President this way
our Larry's got the verve.

In this year of transition
from pandemic and Trump
to a brand new position
coming out of the slump.

So Cambridge bids farewell
and DC says hello
only time will tell
what's next for our fellow

Moving on Again

Studied for many years
even shed some tears
then with PhD in hand
studied for licensing exam

Questions were intense
some made little sense
thought I might fail
till letter came in mail

Congratulating me at last
for I'd actually passed
as Licensed Psychologist
I'd joined a coveted list

Loved working with clients
and the psychology science
thought I'd work forever
remaining very clever

Yet, as it happened
left Miami for retirement
planned to still work
that wasn't how it went

For nearly eight years
I've kept my license alive
yet it's noted by my peers
a new practice didn't arrive

So made the decision
to let license go
met little derision
time is in the flow

Some sadness is mine
but freedom also reigns
I'll set my design
in other worthy domains

No Good Deed

Seller's Remorse

Save us from the co-op board
reigning in New York City
their strangling controlling cord
is really not so pretty

We're prisoners of their crazy whims
we languish while they quibble
hope for selling sooner dims
will the buyer want to nibble

While these nasty members sit
we are left out here dangling
and the buyer may soon quit
as we wait upon their wrangling

Cast Aside

Heart and mind
who's in charge?
whirling thoughts
cascading feelings

Others say walk away
free your soul
they can have their say
but I'm not feeling whole

Defriended
Upended
Cast aside

Others say
let it go
save your pride

But my sadness pervades
as if dark shades
have been drawn

Since she's gone

Memory Lingers

I was completely filled with mirth
to witness this precious rite
for the boy I'd given birth
and on this December night

We gathered to celebrate
with family and friends
he'd picked a perfect mate
and we simply couldn't wait

To accompany him down
the proverbial wedding aisle
when something made me frown
the party planner's act was vile

My cell phone's tiny ring
I quickly tried to disband
only to have her fling
my purse far from my hand

Perhaps this shouldn't matter
but her nasty gesture lingers
did she really need to scatter
leaving me with empty fingers

The evening was divine
and the marriage is still strong
they say forgiveness is fine
and this was a tiny wrong

But though twelve years have passed
and this faux pas is long gone
the memory still sends a cast
sometimes in early dawn.

Family Unrest

Your outright rejection
of your aging mama
may be a reflection
of a family drama

Which preceded your birth
giving license for cutting
from your home and hearth
effectively shutting

And bolting the door
against any intrusion
nursing what's sore
shunning inclusion

Of possible healing
and finding a way
of protecting your feeling
while learning to sway

And discover a path
toward renewed compassion
dispensing with wrath
developing a fashion

For letting your heart
accept an injection
of a healthy new start
toward a loving direction

Baby Talk

We listen with rapt attention
to baby's first words
celebrating every utterance
anything she'll mention

We're completely in awe
we never interrupt
or hurry her along
we don't look for a flaw

Why do we let go of
being so enthralled
with every pearl she shares
when do we shift our love

To hear what it is we say
insisting that she listen
to our parental statements
when is that fateful day

We forget our earlier glee
when her every single word
was absolutely precious
we say "you listen to me!"

Dorothy's Wisdom

December 6, 2008
Larry and Daphna avowed
they'd found the perfect mate
we watched and we were wowed

Friend, Dorothy's words still ring
"A power couple are these two"
they'll both do great things
her prophecy came true.

Daph's a tenured professor
at Harvard Law, no less
Larry's a White House lawyer
much pride I must confess

And to add to the glory
we add Isabella and Nate
they flesh out this story
and we cannot wait

For all that will transpire
as this family grows
setting the world on fire
as only heaven knows

How Dorothy had it right

as we celebrated

that December night

her words were no doubt fated.

Long Term Headache

Nothing can be more of a bear
than trying to get money
out of Long Term Care

So much money we have paid
for the many promises
the company had made

We were so at ease knowing
we had planned so well
we were simply glowing

Never doubting the intention
of a company's promises
surely not a mention

Of doors slammed in our faces
rules we'd not heard of
or the many useless paces

Just to file a claim

Empty Chairs
at Empty Tables

For Sharon Wendt Wesch

Your effervescent light
shines through
forever

A true pioneer
genius not only of the mind
but of the heart

Such a combination
an articulate master of healing

Integrating your intellect
with your soul's heart

Always discovering
new ways to help
heal souls at all levels

Divining the divine
in all your work
and play

Radiant light of our time
what a joy it was
to know you

and learn from you
and with you

If ever there is a person
lighting up the heavens
It is you.

Living in a Strange World

Where is the man I married?
Where is the life we led?
All of these years we carried
The reality of how we're wed

Now his recollections
No longer mesh with mine
Mutual life reflections
Hang from different vines

I'm trying to quell my heart
As I fear it is breaking
Can't I recapture the start
And still this inner quaking

Home used to be an oasis
Where we were always okay
Can I face this new basis
Of changing day by day?

Going...

Broken heart
alone
best friend
Going

Still apparently
here
yet each day
Going

Hiding tears
panic
feeling lost
Gone

Leaving

One by one they're

leaving

I'm alone here

grieving

As these years we're

aging

friends exit with no

staging

So many without

warning

in wee hours I'm

mourning.

As I sit here

writing

I long for one more

sighting

How Can It Be?

He's passed you say
alone at home
without a soul
to hold his hand

I'd not have known
until I searched
phones disconnected
Gmail returned

How can it be
he's gone from me
as we'd just have
entered year fifty-three

Of conversation
about the world
about his kids and mine
a wavelength shared

Through decades
how to explain the
sense of loss
interruption of connection

Yet I'll reach
into the spirit world
and find him there
my friend, Bob Baer

For Bob Pimm on the Death of His Father

He held your little hand
when you came into the land
watched you grow and learn
celebrated every turn

He was clever with his words
and his smile was broad and wide
together you and he
brought about much revelry

He conquered many ills
with abundant skills
his ebullient laughter
will ring forever after

And though he's left this earth
the sparkles of his worth
through particles of light
will shine ever so bright

Little Sister

I'm 74 years old now
you died at 26
why do I still see
you as older than me?

What was it like to be you
so anxious day to day
you still loom large in my eyes
I cannot forget our family ties

You never reached thirty
decades were lost to you
yet I know you can see still
As my life continues to fill

But 26 to 74 is
a complete lifespan
as your little sister I feel
stuck atop the Ferris wheel

Round and round I go
without my big brother
to me you still remain
a force and I can feign

A vision of you as older
in the progression of our years
perhaps as your soul goes on to sail
beyond life's transparent veil

For I'll always see you as the older
the one who's really wiser
despite actual chronology
something in my psychology

Keeps the distance
between our ages

Lost SFWA Voices (South Florida Writers Association)

For nearly twenty years
I've loved sharing with my peers
their writing and mine
some utterly divine

Amid all the voices
we've lost some choices
as they've left our earth
we miss their vast worth

The plays of Dorothy White
were really full of light
for excellent poems we'd look
to Gonny Van den Broek

Margaret McLaughlin
and Lynn MacKinnon
gave of their time
in prose and rhyme

Barbara Weston's words
like songs of birds

lit up my heart
from the very start

Louis Lowy I briefly knew
loved his words too
as his writing
could be exciting

Amid David Miller's prose
the words he carefully chose
of our world's trouble
could make us all bubble

Loved One Losing Memory

Dwindling

losing

finding

fading

reappearing

Sadness

hope

panic

denying

accepting

Heartbreak

wishing

caring

lonely

searching

Remembering

forgetting

questioning

failing

sweetness

Seeking

wanting

All of this to

not be true

Sad Soul

Loneliness

missing

the man

I used to know

Still loving

You now

but I

miss the old you

Heartfelt hurts

tears well

longing

for yesterday

Who am I

in this

sad place

without the you

You once were?

Because I Knew You

For Barry Morris

October 16, 1969
brother Michael's birthday
but I wasn't feeling fine
and needed just to say

I wasn't up to par
sharing brown bag lunch
my thoughts were afar
from our psychology bunch

for you see this birthday
my brother was not here
what can I say
he'd died in spring of that year

yet on this October day
Barry Morris heard of the madness
that stole Michael away
and listened to my sadness

Barry offered me a friendship
that has lasted all these years
we discovered a kinship
beyond that day's tears

as I mourned my brother

Barry offered me his ear

his heart is like no other

and he is so very dear

Barry came into my life

at such a pivotal time

through goodness and strife

from our twenties through our prime

the present madness we face

is a world gone insane

much of the human race

has lost a sense of grace

but I have much gratitude

for my Barry's insights

he's not one for platitudes

as we mourn our lost rights.

For Stephanie Carter

The usual professor of psych testing
Was leaving UM for one year
Dr. Garwood was simply suggesting
I teach his courses to advance my career

Perhaps it was her intention
And vision for what was to come
That her intervention
Would bring a lifelong chum

It was clear from the beginning
In a sparkling shining star
Stephanie Carter was winning
For what there is no bar

She's spiritually aligned
She's compassionate and warm
I've rarely known her kind
She's way above the norm

Meeting Again

Fleeting intensity of
romance at fourteen
ended so soon
youth mourned the
break up as New Year
dawned.

Finally put aside
as a keepsake
yet memories never faded

The heart turned to others
and years became decades
many more lives came about
in the shards left by that one

Earned degrees, pursued vocation
married once for short while
and then again for true love
had children and grands
time filtered through
legendary grains of sand

And now as are all
in the proverbial

autumn of our lives
finding a sweet reunion
where memories recall the
traces of young love

What has remained and
found new life is the core
of the friendship as we recall
strands of The Sidewalks of New York
and remembered September

Words Interrupted

All at once
nigh fifty years
of talking

I cannot call
from my car
and connect

Though you were far
in measured miles
a voice command

To call Bob Baer
and you were there

You seemed to light up
when you heard
it was me

Now lengthy drives
Seem much longer

It's beyond reason
not to hear you
every season

your abrupt passing

leaves me with

words lingering

On my tongue

a heart filled

with longing

For just one more call

Who Is, Was Barry Kaplan?

Fellow traveler on a
journey of light
a trusted soul
a friend, through
it all.

Never afraid to search
for meaning both inner
and beyond.

A kind bear of a man
a sensitive tender
loving persona.

Shared values
compassionate, a man
of integrity.

A mensch for
all seasons
and ever aware

of being true
to self and to
family in all

that entails.

Always
reaching for
decency
respect
caring
loyalty

I'll miss
accessing him
on the physical plane

And now it is time
to invite his
soul to merge

With mine
bringing me messages
from the next dimension.

Tales of Lee and Me

We sat enchanted at
the Hungarian Rendezvous
feasting on delicate
palachinka
sipping tea made from leaves
not tea bags

Two friends sharing
our deepest feelings
a boy and a girl
like brother and sister
but more

Safe to share confidences
about those who'd once loved us
and those who no longer did

Secure in the knowing
our secrets were safe
with one another

The memory of a sweet setting
as we dined on delicate pancakes
and dared to be
fragile with each other

Corner of My Heart

Remembering . . .

The heart knows no endings
though life's turns and bendings
might give the impression
of old love's recession

The love of my youth
still holds a great truth
in the corner of my heart
though years we're apart
I turn over the page
entering older age
there's still a warm place
of remembered embrace

This heart of mine expands
through time's passing sands
sending deep affection
to one whose connection

Is never forgotten

Sweetness

Little Billie runs eagerly to us
without hesitation
shares her embrace
with such dedication

Is there anything
more delicious
than the tiny arms
of one so precious?

This grandchild divine
and she's really all mine
well, she's all ours
with her magical powers

She transforms the atmosphere
with her smiling happy cheer
and even when at times she cries
our hearts expand beyond normal size

This tiny little girl
is full of love and light
she's captured our souls
she's everything that's right!

Dining on Friendship, 2022

I drive down A1A
mostly every Friday
to savor lunch with
Linda, Vashti and Kay
My heart swells with light
the day is so bright
Panera awaits
merriment is in sight
Our souls know a kinship
beyond merely friendship
no topic's off limit
we speak at a fast clip
Hours pass quickly by
I can't tell you why
we eat and we talk
conversation is high

Grandpa and Daddy

To me they were Grandpa and Daddy
Others knew them as Sam and Jimmy
One more shy
One more out there
both filled my young heart
making me feel so safe and happy

Grandpa smoked a pipe
And painted fine art
In the years of his retirement
He'd been a fine lawyer
Before I was born
I still smell the oils
Filling canvases

Daddy wrote for the newspaper
And never retired
'Twas those cigarettes
Which felled him before his time
And the loss of his son
And the sale of the Post
Which stole him away from this earth

Panera Ladies Update

Over three years have passed
since our group started meeting
much dye has been cast
we're still found seating

On Fridays for lunch
the numbers of us
have become a whole bunch
without any fuss

We started as Linda, Holly, and Kay
then Vashti arrived on the scene
so many of us must have our say
and share everything in between

We still speak of energy
and souls here and there
we celebrate synergy
go wherever we dare

One Linda has moved
back to her home in the West
a next Linda has proved
we're constantly blessed

To welcome new faces
who love to explore
lots of beautiful spaces
filling our souls' deepest cores

Jennifer, Anne, and Janeen
are very often among
those who are seen
in our lively throng

And Debra comes when she can
as do others from time to time
metaphysics attracts our clan
we never run out of the rhyme

Panera is where we are found
deepening our connection
and often we end our round
sharing some yummy confection

Some Enchanted Evening

Was It Chance?

Was it fate

On the May date

When you appeared?

A chance meeting

An easy greeting

An easy chat about this and that

No plan in the offing

Just two people scoffing

About flying palmetto bugs

We were not suspicious

Of how this was a propitious

Moment in time

Aha one defining

Without our divining

Did the guides arrange

Our soul's recognition

Of the other's

As our eyes danced together?

The Love of Robert

From the first
we conversed
something opened in me
and in he.

He, tall, thin and charming
totally disarming
his soft brown eyes
made my spirit rise

I readily intuited
this man was wise
more than just smart
a true mensch,
he captured my heart

All these years ago
awakened such a glow
electricity began to flow
and its circuits still grow

He's adored by the kids
and his many friends
the cat knows he's the best
as she lies on his chest

Do You Know?

Do you know you're my inspiration
my muse, my support, my soulmate?
without you my world would lack affirmation
and I would be in a sorry state

Without so much as a fair warning
when I hear your key in the lock
or see your face in the morning
my heart turns over with a knock

It's been this way since the lunch in June
in the year 1975
your presence causes me to swoon
and renders me happy to be alive

Our Story

For nearly forty-six years
through laughter and tears
we've loved each other

Much joy, some sorrow
yesterday and tomorrow
we've spent good times together

In so many ways
we've filled our days
we're really birds of a feather

Perhaps these new rhymes
are as old as times
they tell our story

Meant to Be

There was no maybe
I wanted your baby
almost as soon as we met

Your warmth with your Jill
gave me a thrill
I knew you'd be a great dad

Took a bit of trying
but soon we were flying
Larry was on the way

He was such fun
wanted another one
and so came Andrew

Now the best part
which warms our hearts
is how Jill, Larry and Andrew

Are such good friends
To the living ends
as adults they really are bonded

Somewhere Out There

Pandemic Panic

Endemic of a
pandemic is
the isolation
of a nation

Masking
distancing
no singing

Unless alone
life standing still
gives us a chill

So many dying
the rest trying
to stay safe

New vaccine
arrives on the scene
bringing hope?

Caught in frantic
government antic
scrambling for your turn

Websites crash. Frustration builds. Increasing panic!

Friends competing

for a shot that's fleeting

even a rock concert's seating

Easier to obtain

racking our brains

will we ever again

find life that's sane?

Florida Peril

Because of evil DeSantis
Florida may fade like Atlantis
without mask protection
the spread of infection
will soon send our precious kids
over the proverbial skids

Pandemic Love

When it started
we were all aghast
how long would it
really last?

Trapped at home
none dared to travel
or go to diners
would our minds unravel?

Yet it's apparent
when the world
slowed down
and we couldn't roam
around the town

Couples flourished
and finally found
their unique bonds
beneath the cover
finding each a perfect lover

Night Frights

Virus keeps churning
California's burning
country is turning
what am I discerning?

In late night hours
my mind cowers
hypochondria flowers
I forget my healing powers

A cough from post-nasal drip
an achy back, such a pip
I know I must get a grip
mind rockets at fast clip

Symptoms late at night
produce Covid fright
am I losing sight
getting more uptight

Somehow, writing this down
assuages my constant frown
I'll stop scratching my crown
so I don't have to drown

Deliver Us from Evil

Virus, Violence,

so is this shaky time

we're vulnerable

to all the vile

Vicissitudes of

these moments

Hardly able

to catch our

breath before

the next blow

To our sense

of stability

shocking our sensitivities

shoving us off

Our equilibrium

keeping us on edge

hard to trust

in truth as

we're fed terror

from Trumpists

Who threaten

our existence

with their vivid

assault on all

We await vaccines

From the virus

And veracity

In this turbulent time

When will it come?

Criminal Neglect

In the wee hours of an August morning
learned of an old friend's wife's death
could hardly even catch my breath
till evening fell and another friend with scant warning

Succumbed to Covid-19, the plague of our time
even though he'd had the vaccine
the Delta variant, virulent bug
laid him low, the result of the crime

Of those who make a mockery of human rights
by refusing to get the shots, wear the masks
claiming government can't dictate to them
leaving the vulnerable within our sights

To suffer in hospitals isolated and alone
attended by overworked medical personnel
who've spent too many long months
helpless, listening to those on the phone

Saying goodbye to parents and children
as their lives are suddenly curtailed
and the virus continues to mutate
while so many of our fellow countrymen

Refuse the important injections
listening to liars on Fox News
thus neglecting their responsibility
to stem the tide of these infections

Blind Sight

A full year
saw not one
child or grandchild
COVID fear
invisible tyrant

Your invasion
crossed the world
kept us inside
our masked face
cut off the populace

Shut eateries
silenced Broadway
and concerts

I shied away
from stores
and anywhere
the bug could strike

We Zoomed
we watched Netflix
had food delivered

As weeks became
months and seasons
passed and we

Longed to see
friends and family
to feel the touch

Share a hug
missed grand baby
milestones and
changes

The year 2020
ironically, we lost
vision of each other

And I ask
how can it be?

Empty Ships

Once there were cruises to nowhere
the ships sailed away from the shore
and we could go without a care
for fun, frolic and even more.

A sultry evening spent at sea
reggae music played by the pool
relaxation the promised key
celebration the only rule

Or voyages might be a week
some maybe even much longer
wherever we might care to seek
we returned home that much stronger

Lonely cruise vessels set adrift
with just a mere skeleton crew
we cannot dream about the lift
no more for us the ocean blue.

My envied, sparkling ocean view
in this most popular seaport
where pandemic has set askew
sea vacations no longer sport

I gaze upon these mighty ships
meandering away from shore
passengers have cashed in their chips
there's no one basking anymore.

Hugging

The hugs we missed
for over a year
now newly exist
very sweet and so dear

Hearts to hearts
warmest of embraces
barely pull apart
see joy in our faces

Filling the deep places
where loneliness reigned
we're no longer sad cases
happiness is regained

Holidays, 2020

Who will be going to see
festive holiday windows
or glimpse Rockefeller's tree

Instead of the skating rinks
or the roasted chestnut sales
we'll be enjoying our drinks

Ever still sitting at home
toasting each other on Zoom
not chancing perils to roam

New Year's

Perfect vision
is 2020?
now brings derision
and not aplenty

Rather a blur
overflows our dikes
constant murmur
of COVID spikes

Government fails
to save the many
they're off the rails
truly uncanny

The year now done
turn our sights to
2021
greet the new sun

Missing Grandchildren

The pandemic lingers
its end not in sight
I'm clenching my fingers
as this poem I write

My heart truly aches
for grandchildren to hold
missing them surely takes
me into some cold

Lost, lonely places
of sadness and gloom
I need to see their faces
right here in my room.

Three Pandemic Haiku

Social distancing
group of pelicans swoop by
we yearn for freedom

Meetings with loved ones
on Facebook, Zoom and the phone
longing for their hugs

Cat stares at us
why don't we leave her
to nap on her own?

Politics and Poker

Time to Go

Trump better
go into hidin'
make way now
for President Biden

Pack his things
cut the tweets
no more whining
or rallies and meets

Stop lawsuits
cede the election
exit stage left
follow direction

Far from us
inside a jail
and for this skunk
set highest bail

No Reason

The psychopath and the sycophants
and the Kool-Aid drinking cult
band together
birds of a feather
and nary an adult

In every possible direction
though they still insist that it's rigged
they've lost
this election
we wonder what they've swigged

There is simply no rhyme or reason
for their constant myopia
must still be
the season
to be a Trump dopia

Miscounts

Republicans are

Reprehensible

Repulsive

Rogues

Tearing apart
they have no heart
they're really not smart

Each call to recount
won't change the amount
even as they flout

Their egos are battered
they'll leave us tattered
in the end what has mattered

While attacking the vote
following a treasonous goat
they're sinking the boat

They'll most likely drown
following a clown
as they're run out of town

Balance Restored

Written after Georgia runoff results

It's as if
as it teetered
menacingly
towards its doom

The Titanic was
suddenly righted by
an enormous school
of whales and dolphins

And saved from
the frozen depths
giving time for
the engineers
to repair the hole

Eve of Election, 2024

Waiting waiting waiting
on thin ice we're skating
what will be the choice
when America sounds her voice?

In this endless election
I reach for confection
to soothe my anxious soul
hearing poll after poll

Standing on the brink
what are we to think
whatever happens next
at least they'll stop the texts

No matter how much I give
does money fall thru a sieve?
this old mammala
has given much to Kamala

We will celebrate her win
and cancel all this extra spin
we'll breathe a sigh of relief
as Kamala becomes Chief

Day After Election, 2024

Weepy weepy old me
in all that I can see
my country 'tis of thee
I fear we've lost the key

Will our Democracy
really cease to be?
can we ever be happy
with the rise of tyranny?

I gaze out upon the sea
my heart so very heavy
as our America comes to be
taxed with the Trump legacy

Of promised misery
no more the land of the free
we'll need a new bravery
not give in to slavery

Inauguration Day, 2025

Sing a song of kings
this Trump is many things
mostly he's so very vile
from his fake orange hair
to his insincere smile

Pomp and circumstance
may send us into trance
as we listen to his zeal
and what it does reveal

I lament this infamous day
as American promise goes astray
leaving our hearts hollow
what more is to follow?

Loss of Reason

A country run by a mafioso hood
whose egomania knows no good
rains down destruction
defies reasoned deduction

How this criminal got re-elected
after all the years we've been affected
in every season
amid his acts of treason

If you sing the MAGA anthem
I scratch my head trying to fathom
what's become of your common sense
aren't you even a little tense?

American Pope

At last we have an American pope
To help offset the American dope
Who has us hanging by a rope
With more than we can truly cope

Seasons of Love

Gifts of Gratitude

Counting blessings instead of sheep
Certainly helps me fall asleep
I borrow that expression
As I begin this session

So many reasons
Fill up my seasons
A family of darlings
Each one a starling

Living by the ocean
Fills me with sweet notions
Vast friendships fill me to the brim
So many numbers of hers and hims

In thinking of gratitude
I must take some latitude
Watched Zoe from so young
Till now she has sprung

To remind me of inner knowing
As my health she's sowing
Her counsel has me walking
Correcting my self-talking

Clearing out the cobwebs
As lower back pain ebbs
Healing me from kvetching
She's teaching me some stretching

Beyond imagination
I've rediscovered meditation
Her holistic direction
Reawakens my reflection

Of the Holly I used to be
Taking time and care of me

Never Lost

Everything happens for a reason
whatever way comes the season
though sometimes we feel burned
when we've twisted and turned.

Opening our souls and hearts
even when someone departs
cannot fully erase
the importance of their place

It's really just perception
when we lose direction
and fail to find the gift
even though we may feel miffed.

Just because some situations
bring momentary palpitations
I needn't throw black paint
and only see the taint.

In gratitude for goodness and love
Spirit surrounds us as an ethereal glove
we fill ourselves with light
and resist the urge for flight

Avoiding simple platitude
I still am filled with gratitude
you're still a shining star
and I'll love you from afar.

Twelve Days and Nights...

A jewel arising out of the depths
An oasis in a sea of uncertainty
A magical journey beyond measure

Three aligned souls
Captivated by an essence
Of pampered ecstasy

Soaking up kindness
Sunlight, luxury of luminous
Comfort, filling ourselves with

A ship's offerings
Sipping delicate wine
Dining on exquisite

Imaginative offerings
Served with serenity
And sparkling grace

Days of respite from
Years of unrest
Turbulence, and challenge

Twelve days and nights

Psoriasis Bane

Psoriasis you're surely a bane
You cause me much psychical pain
I don't mean to constantly bitch
about this unseemly itch

At first, ultra-red light seemed to soothe
and render my skin once more smooth
yet this ceased to be my salvation
I can't even get a vacation

For some this disease comes in flares
for me it is always right there
nothing allows it to wane
I fear it may drive me insane

I've applied those various creams
it's only in my best dreams
I get a lasting reprieve
and no longer need to receive

Ongoing torture of new found bumps
popping up on my arms, legs and rump
my skin which was once so serene
I keep it completely unseen

Skin blemished with red blotches and scales
I'm in psoriasis quales
systemic meds' side effects
are something I must reject

it is my most fervent intention
for a future intervention
to eventually come my way
and give me a much brighter day

addendum

When I stopped claiming this as mine
And set it apart
from my mind and my heart
The itch dropped away from the vine

Call to the Medium

Beyond the veil
you're guided
not divided
you know they're there
waiting, waiting

No time for abating
we're here for you stating
go forward with no fear
we love you, my dear

It's your calling
no more stalling
time to recognize
try this on for size

It's one of your gifts
and as you reach out
your words will bring lifts
there'll be little doubt

Time to leave sideline
come into the sunshine
the portals open wide
you'll be able to glide

To gain understanding
don't wait by the landing
you'll see what it's worth
when others greet you with mirth

For decades you've been told
to come into our fold
no more detaining
it's been years of training

Acknowledgments

I celebrate my long and fulfilling relationship with Robert, my husband of a half century in this second volume of poetry he has urged me to publish.

My friends, many of whom have poems dedicated to them, have been a wonderful audience over the years every time I write another poem.

My muse which prompts me to write at all hours of the day and night. I describe this as having poems fall out of me.

Always, Pat Gallant Weich who continues to help me fine-tune my poetry.

Julie Goldsmith Gilbert sparked my motivation to bring out a second poetry book.

Three wonderful children and their spouses, and five divine grandchildren inspire much of my writing.

Dina Rubin spent many hours editing my manuscript and was a delight to work with.

About the Author

Holly W. Schwartztol is a writer, spiritual medium, teacher and a retired psychologist. She is the daughter of James A. Wechsler, a well-known journalist of the 20th century.

Holly has accomplished many things. She obtained her Ph.D. in Counseling Psychology from the University of Miami in 1981. She had an active private practice in Miami for 30 years. She was a school psychologist with Dade County Schools from 1973–1984 and was Co-Director of the Miami Institute of Clinical Hypnosis from 1986–1993. She taught Psychological Assessment for one year at the University of Miami, and some of her students from that time became lifelong friends. Holly was editor of *Transcending Limits*, a newsletter about metaphysics. She was also Co-Founder and Co-Director of MIEL, a holistic center in Miami in the 1990s. She was very active in the field of psychology and was President of many professional organizations, including the Dade County Psychological Association, the Florida Society of Clinical Hypnosis and others. She is also a past president of the South Florida Writers Association.

All of these experiences find expression in Holly's writings.

Holly writes prose, fiction and poetry. She and her parents, James and Nancy Wechsler, wrote a book chronicling the life, mental illness and subsequent suicide of her brother, Michael Wechsler. *In A Darkness* was published first in 1972 and then as a second edition in 1988. It has been instrumental in psychiatric training programs.

Holly trained for many years to be a professional medium and has a private practice on Zoom. She is able to help folks all over the world connect with loved ones who are no longer on earth. All her novels touch on these aspects.

Holly teaches her memoir writing classes on Zoom as well. These Zoom classes are a positive outcome of the very difficult years of the pandemic when people were separated from in-person experiences.

Some glimpses into Holly's writing process:

Holly finds poems tend to present themselves to her and she has to write them down immediately, sometimes in the middle of the night.

She never makes an outline when writing fiction; rather she follows the dictates of her characters and they lead her toward plot development.

Holly consults with other authors, encouraging them to find their unique voices, and she is a very popular teacher of memoir writing.

In 2005, Holly's first novel, *Sherry and the Unseen World*, was published; her second novel, *What We Tell*, came out in 2012; and her third novel, *Coming Around Again*, in 2019, in which the main characters, Sherry and Rosie, from the first novel reappear. Her first volume of poetry is called *Along My Garden Path: Poems on the Rhythms of Life* and was published in 2020.

Holly and her husband live in Central Florida and have three children and five grandchildren. Holly likes to sing, read, do crossword and jigsaw puzzles, play word games from The New York Times, walk, spend time with friends and, of course, write.